# Contents

Any words appearing in the text in bold, **like this**, are explained in the glossary. You can also look out for some of them in the Wet words box at the bottom of each page.

# Rising waters

**Flood fears**

Every year floods affect hundreds of thousands of people around the world. They can cause huge damage. People lose their homes and belongings. Many die or are injured.

It has been raining for days and days. The river is higher than anyone can remember. The ground is soaked. Fields have turned to mud. Water pours down the streets. The drains are overflowing.

It is very dark and quiet outside. The only sound is the splashing of rain on the roof and windows.

A river floods across a road in California, USA, after a storm in January 1999. ▽

# Turbulent Planet

# Wild Water

## Floods

EXPRESS EDITION

Tony Allan

Raintree

**www.raintreepublishers.co.uk**
Visit our website to find out more information about **Raintree** books.

To order:
☎ Phone 44 (0) 1865 888113
▤ Send a fax to 44 (0) 1865 314091
▯ Visit the Raintree Bookshop at **www.raintreepublishers.co.uk** to browse our catalogue and order online.

First published in Great Britain by Raintree Publishers,
Halley Court, Jordan Hill, Oxford
OX2 8EJ, part of Harcourt Education Ltd.
Raintree is a registered trademark of Harcourt Education Ltd.

© Harcourt Education Ltd 2005
First published in paperback in 2005.
The moral right of the proprietor has been asserted.

Produced for Raintree Publishers by Discovery Books Ltd.

Editorial: Charlotte Guillain, Andrew Farrow, Isabel Thomas, Louise Galpine, and Janine de Smet
Design: Victoria Bevan and Ian Winton
Illustrations: Peter Bull and Stefan Chabluk
Picture Research: Rachel Tisdale
Consultant: Keith Lye
Production: Jonathan Smith and Duncan Gilbert
Printed and bound in China by South China Printing Company
Originated by Dot Gradations Ltd, UK

ISBN 1 844 43723 X (hardback)
09 08 07 06 05
10 9 8 7 6 5 4 3 2 1

ISBN 1 844 43728 0 (paperback)
09 08 07 06 05
10 9 8 7 6 5 4 3 2 1

**British Library Cataloguing in Publication Data**
Allan, Tony
Wild water: floods. – (Freestyle express. Turbulent planet)
1. Floods – Juvenile literature
I. Title
551.4'89

A full catalogue record for this book is available from the British Library.

This levelled text is a version of Freestyle: Turbulent Planet: Wild Waters.

**Photo acknowledgements**
p.4/5, Corbis/Philip Wallick; p.5 top, Science Photo Library/ Dr Morley Read; p.5 middle, Corbis/Ecoscene/Sally A Morgan; p.5 bottom, Corbis/Micheal Nicholson; p.6/7, Science Photo Library/Simon Fraser; p.7, Corbis/Patrick Ward; p.8, Corbis/Yann Arthus-Bertrand; p.9, Corbis/ Reuters; p.10, Science Photo Library/Alan Sirulnikoff; p.11, Corbis/Carl & Ann Purcell; p.12/13, Corbis/Caroline Penn; p.12, Corbis Sygma/Bonifacio; p.13, Science Photo Library/ Dr Morley Read ; p.14, Corbis/Charlie Munsey; p.14/15, Corbis/Bettmann; p.15, Science Photo Library/Dr Morley Read; p.16, Science Photo Library/John Mead; p.17, Corbis/Bettmann; p.18/19, Corbis/Ecoscene/Sally A Morgan; p.18, Corbis/Cordaiy Photo Library/Chris North; p.19, Corbis/Lloyd Cluff p.20/21, Corbis/Eye Ubiquitous/Julia Waterlow; p.20, NHPA/Daniel Heuclin; p.21, Corbis/ Wolfgang Kaehler; p.22/23, Corbis/Micheal Nicholson; p.23, Science Photo Library/Douglas Faulkner; p.24, Corbis; p.24 left, Corbis/Connie Ricca; p.25, Corbis; p.26/27, AFP/Getty Images; p.27, JEWEL SAMAD/AFP/Getty Images; p.28, Corbis/Stocktrek; p.28 left, Corbis Sygma/Bill Alkofer; p.29, Corbis/Jacques Torregano; p.30/31, Corbis/Patrick Robert; p.30, Corbis Sygma/Silva Joao; p.31, Corbis Sygma/Las Vegas Sun/Sam Morris; p.32, Corbis/Reuters/Edy Regar; p.33, Corbis/Bisson Bernard; p.33 right, Corbis/Icone Films/Gilles Fonlupt; p.34, Science Photo Library/Andy Harmer; p.34 left, Corbis/Kent News & Picture; p.35, Corbis/Eye Ubiquitous/Jex David Cole; p.36/37, Corbis/Charles E. Rotkin; p.37, Corbis; p.38/39, Philip Gould; p.39 top, Science Photo Library/NASA/ Goddard Flight Center; p.39 bottom, Corbis/FK Photo; p.40/41, Corbis/George H H Huey; p.40, Science Photo Library/NASA/R B Husar; p.41, Corbis Sygma/Telegram Tribune/Jason Mellom; p.42/43, Chromosohm/Joseph Sohm; p.42, Corbis Sygma/Kent News & Picture; p.43, Corbis/Robert Essel NYC; p.44, Corbis/Micheal Nicholson; p.45, Corbis/Reuters/Edy Regar.

Cover photograph reproduced with permission of Topham/Picture Point

Every effort has been made to contact copyright holders of any material reproduced in this book. Any omissions will be rectified in subsequent printings if notice is given to the Publishers.

**Disclaimer**
All the Internet addresses (URLs) given in this book were valid at the time of going to press. However, due to the dynamic nature of the Internet, some addresses may have changed, or sites may have changed or ceased to exist since publication. While the author and Publishers regret any inconvenience this may cause readers, no responsibility for any such changes can be accepted by either the author or the Publishers.

## Find out later . . .

. . . how floods are caused.

. . . how floods can sometimes be helpful.

. . . what people do to stop floods.

## Water power

Suddenly the lights go out. There is no electricity. The telephone lines are dead. Outside, the water level is rising fast. Muddy water is coming in under the door. It is beginning to fill the room. There is just enough time to get upstairs. You must hurry to keep above the rising water. The floods have arrived.

# Wild waters

## Flood areas

Some parts of the world are more likely to flood than others. The dark blue areas in the map below show the regions that flood most often.

When it rains or when snow melts, some of the water soaks into the soil. Some is taken in by plants and some **evaporates**. The rest runs off into streams and rivers.

## Water overflows

Most floods happen when there is too much water for the river **channels**. The rivers then overflow their banks. Water spreads out over land that is already soaked. There is nowhere else for the water to run to.

Alaska

Canada

USA

Mount Shasta

California

Grand Canyon

Colorado

Kansas

Mexico

Galveston

Pennsylvania

Mississippi River

Gulf of Mexico

ATLANTIC OCEAN

Hawaiian Islands

Honduras

Caribbean Sea

PACIFIC OCEAN

Ecuador

Peru

Amazon River

Netherlands

France

Italy

Egypt

Nile River

Tigris River

Euphrates River

Brahmaputra River

Huang He

Indus

Ganges

Bangladesh

Chao Phraya River

Vietnam

Red River

Mekong River

Yangtze River

Japan

PACIFIC OCEAN

Somalia

Kenya

Java

Indonesia

Papua New Guinea

South Africa

Australia

N

## Causes of floods

Floods can occur for other reasons.

**Dams** are built to hold back water in **reservoirs**. Sometimes dams give way and water overflows into the valley below.

The sea can easily flood low-lying land. **Hurricane** winds can make seawater **surge** over the coastline. Giant waves called **tsunamis** can drown whole towns and villages.

**Flood barrier**
Almost one-fifth of the Netherlands was once under water. This flood barrier (above) protects flat, coastal lands.

△ This photograph was taken from an aircraft. It shows large areas of flooding.

## River action

A river starts high up in the hills. Water collects in small streams that flow together to make a river. Near the start of the river, the water flows fast. The powerful running water washes away rocks, soil, and plants from the river's bed and banks. This is called **erosion**.

### Kakadu floods

The picture above shows flooding on the flat lands, or flood **plain**, in the Kakadu National Park, north Australia.

This diagram shows the flow of a river from the **source** to ▽ the **mouth**.

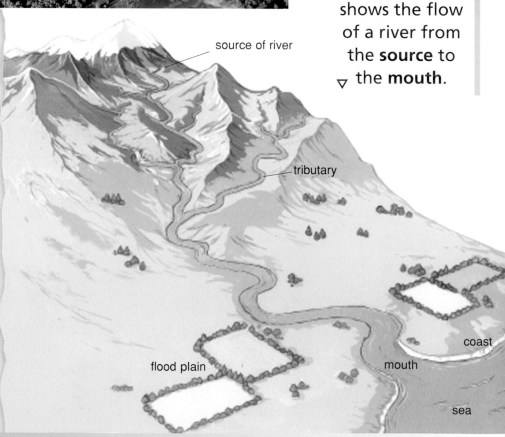

source of river

tributary

flood plain

mouth

coast

sea

**Wet words**   erosion   wearing away of soil or rock by water, wind, and ice

## Down river

As the river flows downstream, the ground begins to flatten out. The river flows more slowly. It cannot carry the larger **particles** but it still holds **silt** and clay. The path of the river bends from side to side.

Over many years it wears away the valley sides, making the land flat. As the river moves to the sea, it drops even the smallest particles. This is called **deposition**. This can cause mud and sand banks to form.

**Seeking safety**
A family (below) are rescued on a raft during floods in Bangladesh in 2000.

particles  small pieces of a substance

## How rain, snow, and ice form

The sun heats up the air and the surface water in oceans, rivers, and lakes. Some of the water turns to **water vapour**. The warm water vapour rises in the air. As it rises, it cools off and **condenses**. It condenses into water droplets or ice **crystals**. The water droplets and ice crystals form clouds. They then fall from the clouds as rain, snow, or hail. This is called **precipitation**.

### Rainbows

A rainbow (below) forms when sunlight enters drops of rain. A rainbow appears as a **spectrum**, or band of colours.

This diagram shows the movement of water from the sea to the air, to clouds, and back to the land.

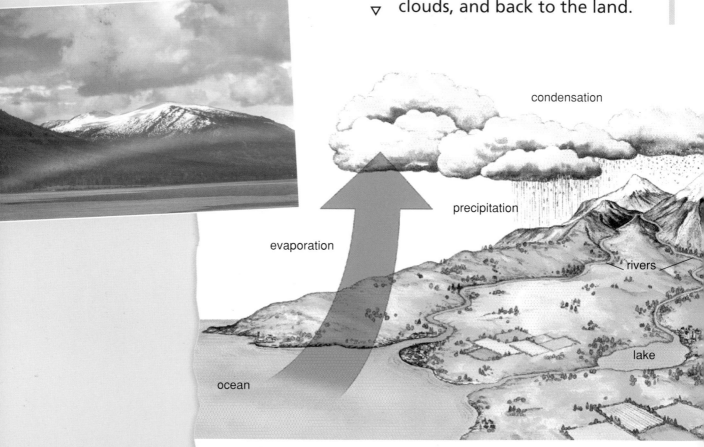

condensation

precipitation

evaporation

rivers

ocean

lake

precipitation   general term for rain, snow, sleet, dew, or hail

## Into the earth

Some rain falls into the seas and oceans. The rest falls on land where it soaks into the soil. This is called **groundwater**.

Plants take up some of this water through their roots. Water also **evaporates** from the leaves of plants into the air. This is called **transpiration**.

**Huang He**
Huang He, or Yellow River, is China's second longest river. In the picture below, it breaks up into several **channels** to pass through a mountain valley.

transpiration    when plants take in water through their roots and give off water vapour through their leaves

11

# When rivers burst their banks

Heavy rainfall is the most common cause of river floods. As rain falls, some soaks into the ground. Eventually, the water level rises too high and the river breaks its banks.

**City water**
If there is too much rain water for drains to cope with, towns and cities may flood (above).

**Wet words**    delta    wide, fan-shaped area of land where a river flows into the sea

## Monsoon floods

Rivers flood all round the world. Some of the worst flooding happens in southern Asia. Winds called **monsoons** bring heavy rains in summer and autumn. In the year 2000, monsoon rains in the Mekong Valley caused terrible floods. Over 4 million people had to leave their homes.

These women are used to floods. The Mekong **Delta** region of ▽ Vietnam is often under water.

### Cutting down forests

Trees help to reduce the risk of flooding. They take up water from the ground as they grow. When they are cut down (below), more water runs into rivers instead .

## Flash floods

Sometimes, very heavy rainfall can make rivers flood their banks in hours. If a river floods soon after rain starts to fall, it is called a **flash flood**. The flood rises and falls very quickly with little or no warning. These floods can be very dangerous. People do not have time to reach safety.

## Fast and furious

In 1999, 44 people were **canyoning** down a river in Switzerland. A sudden **torrent**, caused by a flash flood, killed 19 of them.

### Antelope Canyon

Antelope Canyon (below right) in Grand Canyon National Park, USA, is usually very dry. But in 1997, 11 hikers drowned when a 3-metre (10-feet) wall of water swept them away.

canyoning   sport of climbing and swimming, or rafting in canyons

## Big Thompson Canyon

In 1976, one of the USA's worst flash floods happened in Colorado. A group of people were visiting Big Thompson Canyon.

A terrible storm hit the region. A wall of water flooded down the **canyon**. It killed 139 people.

◁ A rescue worker looks at the damage done by the flash flood at Big Thompson Canyon, USA, in 1976.

### Ecuador flood

Floodwater rushes down the Mazan Valley, high in the Andes Mountains of Ecuador (above). Normally this stream is only 2 metres (6 feet) wide.

## Broken dams

**Dams** are built across streams or rivers to hold back water. They control floods and provide water for people to use. If a dam bursts, it releases great walls of water. These can wipe out everything in their path. Fortunately, such accidents are rare.

embankment dam

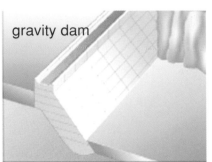
gravity dam

arch dam

buttress dam

Mount Shasta Dam in California, USA, is an
▽ embankment dam.

### Types of dam

There are four main types of dams. **Embankment** dams are used in rivers that have broad valleys. Gravity, arch, and buttress dams are found in narrow valleys.

dam   barrier built to hold back water

## Vaiont Dam, Italy

In 1963, the side of a mountain slid into the **reservoir** behind Vaiont Dam, in Italy. This caused a giant wave 100 metres (328 feet) high.

## Dam disaster

The wave swept over the top of the dam into the valley below. Many villages were completely swept away by the force of the floodwater. About 2500 people were killed.

### Still standing

These shattered houses (below) were hit by the floodwater in the Vaiont Dam disaster in Italy in 1963.

# Helpful floods

We usually think of floods as bad because of the damage they do. But sometimes floods can bring benefits. For hundreds of years, Egypt's River Nile flooded in the late summer. When it flooded, it carried **silt** to the land both sides of the river. Silt contains **nutrients** that help plants to grow well. Better crop harvests were produced.

## Ancient settlements

Many early **settlers** made their homes near great rivers, like the River Tigris in southern Iraq (below). The land was **fertile** so it was easy to grow food.

A canal brings water from the River Nile to fields in Egypt. ▽

nutrient   nourishment

## Floods and food

Today, millions of rice growers in southern Asia depend on floods. They use flooded fields called **paddies** to grow their crops. The best land for paddies is in the flood **plains** of rivers.

### Aswan High Dam

The Aswan High Dam was built across the River Nile (above). The dam helps to control the flow of water to the land. Since it opened in 1971, Egypt's harvest has more than doubled.

---

**paddy**   water-filled field used for growing rice

## Sorghum

The Chinese use a plant called sorghum (below) to help control floods. Millions of bundles are built into the sides of dykes. This helps to stop the riverbank **eroding**.

## The Yellow River

More people live near the banks of the Huang He, or Yellow River, than any other river in China. The land is very **fertile** because of the rich, yellow **silt**.

## Silt and floods

The Huang He floods more than any other river on Earth. This is because the river carries large amounts of silt. The silt sinks to the bottom of the river. This raises the water level of the river.

For hundreds of years, people have built and rebuilt **dykes** to stop the river flooding. In some places the riverbed is 4.5 metres (15 feet) above the **plain**.

The Huang He, or ▷
Yellow River, in China
is 5464 kilometres
(3395 miles) long.

### River deaths

When the Huang He breaks its banks, the floodwater covers a huge area. The farmland becomes more fertile. But the floods also kill people. Almost one million people died when the river flooded in 1887.

### Yangtze River

The rice **paddies** on the banks of China's Yangtze River are built up as **terraces** (below). Terraces stop water draining away after a flood.

terrace   flat area of land cut into a slope

# When the sea floods the land

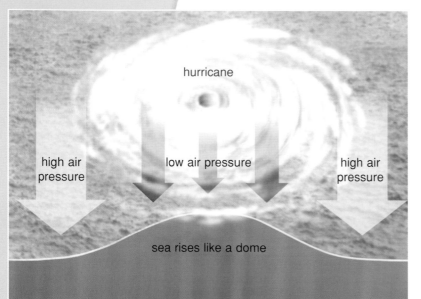

hurricane

high air pressure

low air pressure

high air pressure

sea rises like a dome

A **hurricane** is a huge swirling storm that starts out at sea. Underneath a hurricane the sea level rises like a dome. As the hurricane hits land, the huge amount of water **surges** on to the shore. It can cause terrible floods.

## Dome of water

A dome of water forms under a hurricane out at sea (above). This is because the **air pressure** at the hurricane's centre is lower than the air pressure at its edges.

The Thames Barrier on the △ River Thames in London, England.

**Wet words**     air pressure   force of the air pressing down on the Earth

## The Thames Barrier

Any low-lying area can be at risk from flooding. In 1953, a very bad flood in eastern England killed over 300 people. A barrier was then built across the River Thames. It protects London from flooding at high tide. The barrier can be raised if a flood is expected.

### Storm surge

A storm surge, like the one below, can be caused by a hurricane.

**surge**   sudden rush of water

### Terrifying tsunamis

A **tsunami** is a giant wave. It is caused by an **earthquake**, **landslide**, or volcanic **eruption** on the ocean floor. A tsunami travels through the ocean as a small wave. When it reaches the shore, it rolls up to heights of over 30 metres (100 feet). It can cause terrible destruction.

### Hawaiian Islands

In 1957, a huge earthquake in the Pacific Ocean caused a tsunami. The tsunami hit the Hawaiian Islands. The tsunami caused great damage. Luckily, no lives were lost.

**Stay away!**
Never go to the beach to watch a tsunami arrive. By the time you see the wave, it will be too late to escape.

A tsunami caused these floods at Oahu, one of the Hawaiian Islands. ▽

TSUNAMI HAZARD ZONE

IN CASE OF EARTHQUAKE, GO TO HIGH GROUND OR INLAND

satellite   device orbiting the Earth sent up into space by a rocket

## Tsunami warnings

Today, there are special centres that watch for signs of a tsunami. These centres are near the Pacific Ocean. This is where most tsunamis occur.

Scientists study information from computers and **satellites**. When they detect undersea **shockwaves**, warnings are given out to the areas at risk.

**Alaska, 1964**
An earthquake started a tsunami that struck Alaska in 1964. The tsunami wrecked this oil tanker and fishing boat (below).

shockwave    huge burst of energy released from the Earth during an earthquake

## Indian Ocean, 2004

On 26 December 2004, the strongest **earthquake** for 40 years shook the surface of the Indian Ocean. Waves travelled across the ocean at speeds of up to 960 kilometres (600 miles) per hour. The waves slammed into Indonesia, Thailand, India, and Sri Lanka.

There was no system in the Indian Ocean to watch for tsunamis. The giant waves hit without warning. Many people did not have time to escape.

### Tsunami map

The map above shows the point where the earthquake happened. It shows how far the waves travelled outwards and how many countries they reached.

earthquake   shaking or trembling of the ground

## Major world disaster

The force of the water was huge. The waves washed away buildings, cars, boats, and even cattle. Whole towns and villages were destroyed. Many areas on the coast were turned into wasteland.

Over 250,000 people died in eleven countries. Many people are still missing. The total number of deaths may never be known.

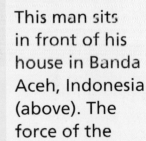

Tourists in Thailand run from the 2004 tsunami as it hits the shoreline. ▽

**Banda Aceh**
This man sits in front of his house in Banda Aceh, Indonesia (above). The force of the water has driven this boat through the middle of his home.

# Surviving a flood

People are getting better at predicting floods. **Forecasters** receive reports from weather stations on the ground. They use **data** from **satellites** to help them. Special aeroplanes track storms that might cause flooding.

A satellite image tracks a **hurricane** in the Gulf of Mexico in 1996.
▽

## Water damage

Floodwater can cause huge damage to people's homes. This man (below) is looking at the water in his son's bedroom.

data   information from an experiment, a survey, or which may be stored on a computer

## Measuring flood risk

Experts use other ways to check for risk of flooding. Special instruments **monitor** rivers 24 hours a day.

The instruments measure the height of the water in the river. They also measure how fast the river is flowing. The machines send the information to computers. Experts study the results. They can then work out the danger level.

### River Seine

These workers (below) are checking the flow of the River Seine in Paris, France. They are looking out for rising water levels.

## Preparing for a flood

If people know that a flood is coming, these are some of the things they do to prepare:

- Make sure they know how to turn off the gas, electricity, and water supply.
- Move belongings to an upper storey of the house.
- When the water enters the house, go to an upper level.

**Quick escape**

This 73-year-old man (below) escaped from a flood by climbing up a tree. A rescue worker helps him to safety.

After storms in ▷ the south of France in 1999, a man waits for rescue on the roof of his flooded home.

## Survival tips

- Never stay in a car. Just 30 centimetres (12 inches) of water can sweep away small cars.
- Do not try to walk through a flood. Fast-flowing water 15 centimetres (6 inches) deep can carry a person away.
- Watch out for fallen power lines. They may be live.
- Try to reach high ground.
- Wait to be rescued.

**Swept away**
A car is not a safe place to sit out a flood. Powerful floods carried off this car (below) in Las Vegas, USA in 1999.

## Keeping alive

After the floods die down, many people may be homeless. Getting help can be difficult if floodwaters have destroyed roads and bridges. Telephone and power lines may also be down.

## No food or water

In poorer countries there is a risk of **famine**. Food crops may have been swept away. Drinking water may be **polluted**. Floodwater can also spread diseases.

### Homeless

In 2003, there were floods in Indonesia. These people (below right) lost their homes after water swept through their village.

famine   extreme lack of food

## No heat or light

The **emergency services** have a huge job to do. Homeless people need shelter, warmth, and food. Damaged gas pipes and electricity cables can cause fires. They need to be repaired quickly.

## Cleaning up

After a flood drains away, it leaves behind a terrible mess. Streets are covered in mud and **debris**. Homes and belongings are ruined by floodwater. Cleaning up can take a long time.

**French Floods**

The Rhône Valley in south-east France is protected from flooding by **dykes**. In 1999, a dyke broke in after heavy storms. Many homes like those below were flooded.

Students in Honduras, Central America help clear up flood damage in 1998.

# Coping with floods

## Be prepared

It is difficult to stop floodwater flowing into people's homes. This man is blocking up a doorway with sandbags (below).

People have always tried to protect themselves from floods by raising the height of riverbanks. They build up the banks with mounds of earth or stone. These are called **embankments** or **levees**. People also build **dams** to control the flow of rivers.

## Looking after the land

Farmers can help to prevent flooding if they look after their land. They can dig ditches to drain water from fields. They can plant trees and bushes. Trees help to slow down the flow of water through the soil. They also take up water through their roots.

Planting trees can ▷ reduce flooding because trees take up water.

embankment   raised barrier along a riverbank, often called a levee

## Getting away

In countries where it floods often, people need to escape fast. They build special shelters. The shelters are on high ground.

### High and dry

This ancient timber house in Thailand stands on high wooden **stilts** (left). This raises the house above the flood level to keep it dry.

stilts   raised legs

## How dams stop floods

**Dams** and **reservoirs** stop floods before they start. Dams hold back the water in reservoirs. When a big storm hits, the gates of the dam are closed. The water in the reservoir rises. When the rain stops the water is let out slowly. The reservoir is now ready for the next storm.

### Tennessee dams

The map below shows the Tennessee, Ohio, and Mississippi Rivers in the USA. A system of dams and reservoirs stops the rivers flooding.

50 miles
50 kilometres

ILLINOIS
Ohio River
KENTUCKY
VIRGINIA
MISSOURI
Fontana Dam
NORTH CAROLINA
ARKANSAS
TENNESSEE
Chickamauga Dam
Hiwassee Dam
Memphis
Mississippi River
Tennessee River
Chattanooga
SOUTH CAROLINA
Wilson Dam
GEORGIA
MISSISSIPPI
ALABAMA
N

Area served by Tennessee Valley Authority

Dams

**reservoir**  artificial or natural lake that stores water for people to use

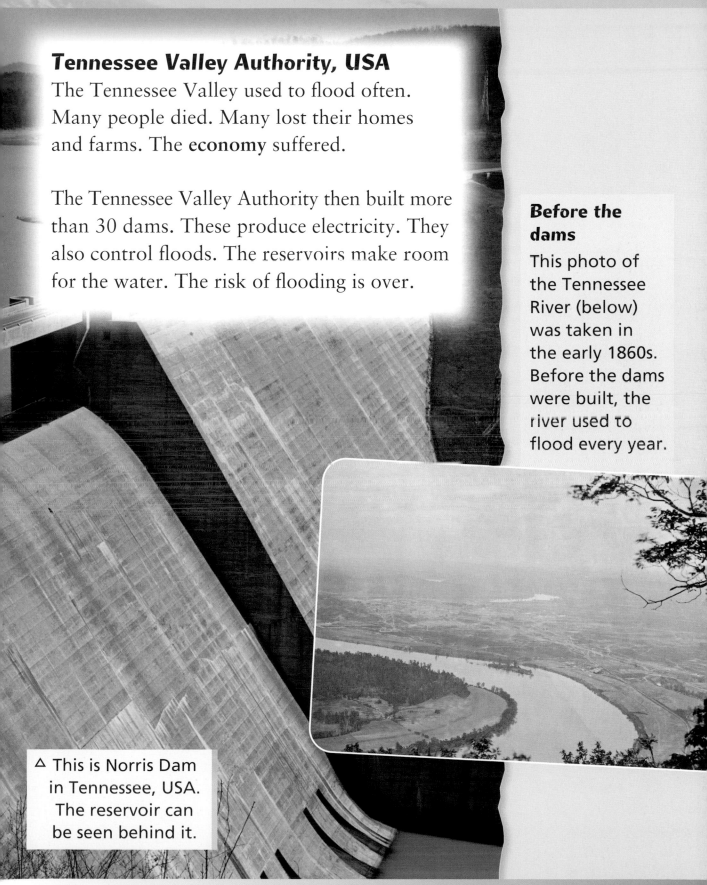

# Tennessee Valley Authority, USA

The Tennessee Valley used to flood often. Many people died. Many lost their homes and farms. The **economy** suffered.

The Tennessee Valley Authority then built more than 30 dams. These produce electricity. They also control floods. The reservoirs make room for the water. The risk of flooding is over.

**Before the dams**

This photo of the Tennessee River (below) was taken in the early 1860s. Before the dams were built, the river used to flood every year.

△ This is Norris Dam in Tennessee, USA. The reservoir can be seen behind it.

economy    business activity of people living in an area

## The Mississippi

The Mississippi is one of the largest rivers in the USA. It carries a greater amount of water than any other river. It also has a history of very bad floods. People built **levees**, but major floods still happened.

## The worst flood

In 1927, the levees broke in 120 places. The floods killed at least 250 people. Nearly 650,000 were driven from their homes. The US government then built **dams**, **reservoirs**, and **diversion channels** to control the river.

### River's course

The map below shows the Mississippi River. It is 3780 kilometres (2350 miles) long. It drains all or part of 31 US states.

MINNESOTA
WISCONSIN
IOWA
ILLINOIS
Mississippi River
MISSOURI
KENTUCKY
TENNESSEE
Memphis
USA
ARKANSAS
MISSISSIPPI
LOUISIANA
New Orleans
MEXICO
500 miles
500 kilometres
Gulf of Mexico
N

diversion channel    channel dug alongside a river to drain floodwater

## Still flooding

The Mississippi is still not totally controlled. Heavy rains in 1993 caused the worst disaster since 1927. Iowa, Wisconsin, Illinois, and Missouri were all badly flooded.

In Louisiana, USA, a flood centre controls how much water reaches the main river when floods are expected. ▽

### Three rivers

This **satellite** image was taken during floods in 1993. It shows where the Mississippi (top left), Missouri (centre), and Illinois (top centre) rivers meet.

# Weird weather

## Seen from space

A **satellite** image of the Earth (below) shows the warm-water current linked to El Niño. It is the red band in the centre next to the Pacific coast of South America.

There is more flooding around the world in some years than others. Places that usually have heavy rain may have **drought**. Scientists think these changes are caused by the El Niño effect.

## What is El Niño?

El Niño is a change in the flow of ocean **currents** in the Pacific Ocean. Normally, the winds and currents flow westwards. They carry warm water away from South America. When the winds and currents change direction, an El Niño event happens. The warm waters come much closer to the coast of South America.

drought   when there is no rain for a long time and water supplies run out

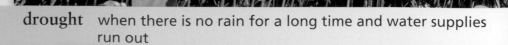

## Different weather

Scientists cannot predict when an El Niño year will happen. When one does occur, winds bring heavy rainfall to the South American coast. This area is usually desert.

On the far side of the world, the opposite happens. Southern Asia usually gets **monsoon** winds and rain. This area is dry.

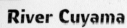

### River Cuyama

In February 1998, El Niño brought heavy rains to California, USA. The aerial picture above shows the flooded River Cuyama in California.

△ This land is normally a desert. Heavy rains have made these flowers grow.

## Are floods getting worse?

The number of floods is going up every year. There were six major flood disasters around the world in the 1960s. There were 18 in the 1980s, and 26 in the 1990s.

## Warmer, wetter world

**Global warming** may be one reason why the number of floods is growing.

People are burning more coal, oil, and other fuels. These send harmful gases into the Earth's **atmosphere**. These gases trap the sun's heat inside the atmosphere. This makes the world warmer and wetter.

### Building over

When an area is built over, rain cannot soak into the soil. The water has nowhere to go. This flooded road (below) has almost turned into a river. It is easier to cycle than to walk!

atmosphere layer of gases that surround the Earth

## Water under control

We cannot stop floods completely. But we are doing more to control them. More **dams** and **diversion channels** are being built. Farmers are managing their land better. People are more aware of the dangers of building houses on the flood **plain**. We need water to keep our planet alive. But we just need to make sure that it is under control.

△ The smoke from these chimneys is sending harmful gases into the atmosphere.

**Wonderful wetlands**

Wetlands, like the one below, are near rivers and coasts. They soak up the floodwater like a sponge.

global warming  warming up of the Earth's climate

43

# Find out more

## Websites

### USA's TV Weather Channel

Search for news, forecasts, and information about weather in the past.

www.weather.com

### BBC Weather

Features, photos, and interesting facts about the weather.

www.bbc.co.uk/weather

### TVA

Useful information about the Tennessee Valley Authority.

www.tvakids.com

## Books

*Disasters in Nature: Floods*
    Catherine Chambers (Heinemann Library, 2000)
*Nature on the Rampage: Floods*
    Tami Deedrick (Raintree, 2004)

## World Wide Web

To find out more about floods you can search the Internet. Use keywords like these:

- floods +[country]
- tsunami +news +[date]
- "El Niño"

You can find your own keywords by using words from this book. The search tips opposite will help you find useful websites.

## Search tips

There are billions of pages on the Internet. It can be difficult to find exactly what you are looking for. These tips will help you find useful websites more quickly:

- Know what you want to find out
- Use simple keywords
- Use two to six keywords in a search
- Only use names of people, places, or things
- Put double quote marks around words that go together, for example "global warming"

## Where to look

### Search engine

A search engine looks through the whole web. It lists all the sites that match the words in the search box. You will find the best matches are at the top of the list, on the first page.

### Search directory

A person instead of a computer has sorted a search directory. You can search by keyword or subject and browse through the different sites. It is like looking through books on a library shelf.

# Glossary

**air pressure**  force of the air pressing down on the Earth

**atmosphere**  layer of gases that surround the Earth

**canyon**  deep, narrow valley, often with a stream running through it

**canyoning**  sport of climbing and swimming, or rafting in canyons

**channel**  groove in the ground that a river or stream runs along

**condense**  turn from gas into a liquid

**crystal**  solid substance with atoms arranged in a regular pattern

**current**  flow of air or water

**dam**  barrier built to hold back water

**data**  information from an experiment, a survey, or which may be stored on a computer

**debris**  bits and pieces of something broken or destroyed

**delta**  wide, fan-shaped area of land where a river flows into the sea

**deposition**  dropping of material by rivers, seas, or winds

**diversion channel**  channel dug alongside a river to drain floodwater

**drought**  when there is no rain for a long time and water supplies run out

**dyke**  long wall of earth built to keep water out

**earthquake**  shaking or trembling of the ground

**economy**  business activity of people living in an area

**embankment**  raised barrier along a riverbank, often called a levee

**emergency services**  police, ambulance, air-sea rescue, and fire brigade

**erosion**  wearing away of soil or rock by water, wind, and ice

**eruption**  sudden force of gas, fire, and ash through the Earth's surface

**evaporate**  turn from liquid into gas or vapour

**famine**  extreme lack of food

**fertile**  allows plants to grow well

**flash flood**  quickly developing flood

**forecaster**  person who works out future weather

**global warming**  warming up of the Earth's climate

**groundwater**  water that soaks into the ground

**hurricane**  huge, swirling storm with winds of more than 118 kilometres (73 miles) per hour

**landslide**  mass of rocks or soil sliding down from a hillside

**levee**  raised barrier along a riverbank

**monitor**  check something regularly

**monsoon**  rainy season in some tropical countries

**mouth**  place where a river flows into the sea

**nutrient**   nourishment

**paddy**   water-filled field used for growing rice

**particles**   small pieces of a substance

**plain**   flat lands

**pollute**   add harmful substances to air, water, or land

**precipitation**   general term for rain, snow, sleet, dew, hail

**reservoir**   artificial or natural lake that stores water for people to use

**satellite**   device orbiting the Earth sent up into space by a rocket

**settler**   person who settles in a new country or place

**shockwave**   huge burst of energy released from the Earth during an earthquake

**silt**   soil particles carried by a river

**source**   place where a river starts

**spectrum**   band of colours as seen in a rainbow

**stilts**   raised legs

**surge**   sudden rush of water

**terrace**   flat area of land cut into a slope

**torrent**   rushing stream of water

**transpiration**   when plants take in water through their roots and give off water vapour through their leaves

**tsunami**   giant wave set off by an undersea earthquake or volcanic eruption

**water vapour**   water in the form of a gas

# Index